ZAYRA YVES

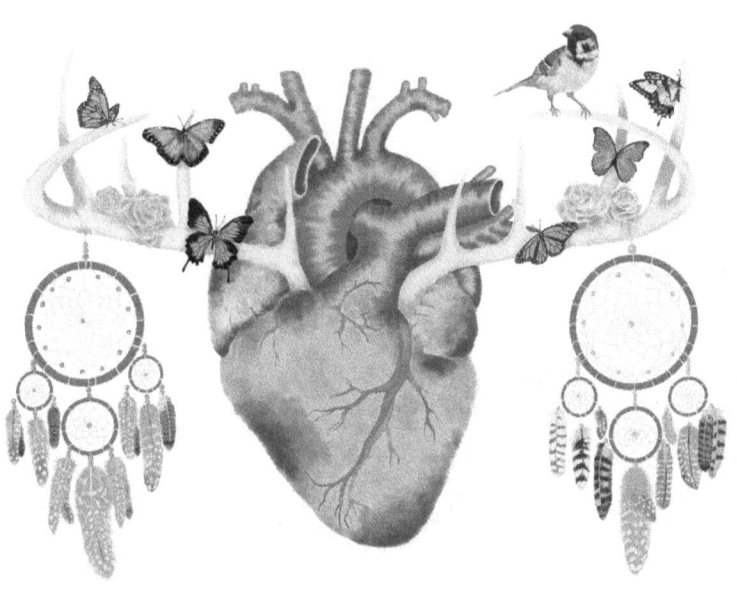

UNEARTHED
Selected Poetry of Zayra Yves

Unearthed
Copyright 2023 by Zayra Yves

All rights reserved. No part of this book
may be used or reproduced by any means,
graphic, electronic or mechanical, including
photocopying, recording, taping or by any
information storage retrieval system without
the written permission of the publisher except
in the case of brief quotations embodied in
critical articles
and reviews.

Contact the author: www.zayrayves.com

Front cover art & Interior art: CB Williams
www.inprint.com/gallery/finiteeve

Photo of Zayra Yves on page 3 by Zayra Yves
Photo of Zayra Yves on back cover by FotobyT

ISBN (Hardcover): 979-8-218-22998-6
ISBN (Paperback): 979-8-218-22999-3

Published by Deep Waters

Poetry Collections:

Empty as Nirvana

Ordinary Substance

Color Me Pomegranate

Leaving You Unpainted

Audio Poetry Collections:

Crowned Compassion

Sleep in the Sea in the Tonight with Me

Lanterns

a new collection: *Come Be My Light*

*Hearts rebuilt from hope
resurrect dreams killed by hate.*

- Aberjhani

In loving memory Bill Jaenike, Erik Campi, Glen Woodward,
Julian Sparrow and all the wild, beautiful travelers we lost to the road.

Table of Contents

Come Be My Light	10
Skyjacked	12
Escape	14
Bee Keeper	15
Another Kind of Purple	16
After…	17
Ash	18
Eating Marigolds…	19
Now I Believe You	20
SUNKISSED WOMAN	21
Clouds	22
The Way I Love is a Liability	23
Acid Love	25
Strings	26
Sand Worship	28
Alone with Confessions	29
Forest Fire	30
Sunflower Tattoos	31
Love's Sanctuary…	32
My Body: A Mermaid Graveyard	34
Survivalist	35
Haunted Waters	36
SIPHONED LIGHT	38
Forbidden City	40
Taking Back the Words	41
The Stuff Indie Films are Made of	42
The Blue Buddha Painting	43
In the Shadow of a Hunter's Moon	44
Don't Send Flowers, Send Dostoevsky	45
My Intricate Hallucination	47
In the Afterglow	48
Telepathy	49

You are a lot like a holiday:	50
When Sundays were all we had...	51
The boundary line...	52
Misplaced Apostrophe	53
Smugglers	54
I Wrote a Prayer for You	55
Suicidal Planets	57
We Want to Be Taken by Surprise	58
The Light in Your Eyes	59
Forgotten Ancestors	60
Spilling	61
Failed Seeds	62
Encounter	64
Ensconce	65
Schizophrenic Swerve	66
Not Equal to the Gods	67
Everlasting	68
For the Love of Oranges	69
Lifeboat	70
Vanquished	71
blue lanterns in midsummer	72
Muses	74
In the Spirit of Ezra Pound	76
One Soul	77
Tobacco	78
You Are My Earth	79
Cineastas	80
Leave the Lamp On	81
San Francisco Jangle	82
Thirst	83
Becoming a Falcon	84
Alabaster	85

Dreamcatcher	86
Lotus in the Mud	87
The Grace Surrounding Us	88
The Journey to Love	89
A love story inside structure of color	90
Fourth Chamber of My Heart	91
Tears of a Pilgrim Poet: Sparrow	93
Soul Means Bird	96
Our Lady of Sorrows	97
Our Hearts Are Listening	98
Naming the Cherry	100
When They Were Seventeen	101
Unabbreviated	102
Gutter Punk	103
Street Monk	104
A Study in Poppies	106
Nine Dragons	107
Another Word for "Mother"	108
Behind Door #9	109
Hobo Cavalcade	111
For the Old Homeless Man	112
Naked Man Smoking in the Alley	113
That Light Which Lights the Longer Light	114
That Break-with-Reality Episode	116
Chanting in Blood Languages	118
Had it Been Water	120
Leave of Absence	121
Prayers at the Crossroads	122
Lost Child	123
Our Lady of the Lost Children	124
This is what I inherited from you...	126
Naked on the Boulevard	127
Nothing Except Opera	129
Illusions of Grandeur	131
Biography of a Stone	133

Slaughter Bone Oracle ... 134
Apocalyptic Angel ... 136
Vacant as the Sky ... 138
One Hundred and One Poems Later ... 139
Floating in the Dark ... 141
Meeting You in Jiangxi ... 142
A Six-Winged Seraph Came to Earth ... 143
may the books of sky open ... 145
Time to Give My Heart Away ... 146
The Song of the Living ... 147
In Search of a Gypsy Love Poem ... 150
By Now the Light has Faded ... 152
The Light the Angels Speak Of ... 153
The Unveiling ... 154
Author's NOTES & ACKNOWLEDGMENTS: ... 156

Come Be My Light

After all this time I know nothing.

I am not certain of friendship
or the color of a loyal soul;
unsure of time,
and lacking faith.

I no longer trust words written
by the advantages
of a unicorn moon, an influencer,
or a tender flower crushed
between the pages
of a holy book.

I suspect this might upset you
but I think nothing of metaphysics,
esotericism
or farewells spoken in vanity
especially from the lips
of those who have named themselves for a goddess,
a chant or the chosen few.

I see ancient faces in their deaths
moaning an elegy, grasping for immortality
the same as a long dream.

Unfeeling, unforgiving
and letting go of no deed:
the particles of matter,
tiny memories
broken by someone's hand
and forgotten

in a swelling sea of humanity.

My inner language
and cherished beliefs in goodness
are eclipsed
and cease to invoke illumination
as I float
in a starless sky,

move silently thru a dark maze of ordinary words,
implying blank spaces
where once I wrote
poetic virtues, unfettered ballads
and wild prose
no less epic
than the generosity
of love.

Some say love never dies
it can only be buried
and wait to be
unearthed.

Come be my light,
come sing
me back to life.

Skyjacked

You should know right from the beginning
that my wings were cut off.

This all happened while someone repeated
over and over in my ear that love is not lyrical.

I cannot overcome my tendency to fall into
M E L A N C H O L Y:

insulted, injured and divorced from fantasy
with wounds that refuse to be aestheticized.

It is equally important that you know
my heart is traceable and can be found.

Every clash of a world-renowned conflict
lives inside this story I am sharing with you.

It's as if the contradictory impulse thrives
in the nest egg and in the death of my freedom.

You have asked yourself if I loved you;
if I loved you a little more than enough.

It's the choice of words. It's the delivery.

It's the details hidden in the nuances and silence.

You should also know that my wings grew back.
It was such a spectacle in it's own right.

All I can say for myself, or loss, or victory,
or even you, is that there's no way to avoid ruin.

Love is what carried me far from you.
Love is what brought me back again.

Escape

Escape
Here, at the edge I climb out of my body
no longer the girl you remember,
and definitely not the same woman you loved.
From where I am standing
not even the gargoyles utter your name.
I won't blame anyone or sing a song about a red moon.
It seems unkind to explain why.
All I know is it is easier to let the colors blend,
it is better this way, that I leave you
before I start to fade.

Bee Keeper

For years I have swallowed the bees you left behind. They never stop mating. Their stingers are lodged in my throat, esophagus, stomach, and spleen. Sometimes they fly out of my mouth in mid-sentence and someone looks at me astonished. They want to know where it came from. How can I be harboring a colony of bees inside of me? Every answer I offer is not the right one, is not believable. Tomorrow I will find a way to explain it is the honey. It is that time in our lives of thick sticky sweetness I cannot let go of and the hexagonal catacomb of my living heart is best suited to keep the hive alive.

Published: Some Voices Sing, An International Anthology of Hope, produced by Blue Catharsis Publishing.
It is available from Bookscrown: https://bookscrown.com/some-voices-sing-anthology-of-hope

Another Kind of Purple

December skies. The feeling of blue before
it touches my skin, washed in winter's colors.

As in, you are here with your hand in mine.
As if, this is only the beginning of love, not the end.

Even when I think of it now, it stings.
How easy it was for you to close out the world,

to shut off the light and roll over saying,
"It's all good, never-mind, I trust you."

The dark doesn't mean much. Always quiet,
full of unknown truths, burdened with mystery.

But I was awake thinking of someone
I used to love. He was a lot like you.

Forgive me for leaving before sunrise
without a word, without a glance.

After...

I had to walk significant distances
across the terrain
of my heart
and keep my eyes open;
watch in all directions to guard
against demons
dressed like wounded saints
and holy people
giving away poisoned waters.

I had to keep the torches lit
along the razor wire
along barriers
I erected
against the invasion
of more petty thieves
like you
who pretend to be kind
and just
but really intend
nothing more than to steal
the best sugar
I've got.

Ash

In a city of gangsters and flamethrowers
you break my heart, slash the face of a girl,
hurl poetry against the wall and let the words bleed out.

You imagine the blue lights won't reach me,
that your fingerprints will wash off,
and my body won't remember.

I think to myself how interesting it must have been
for you to become the demon,
so smug as I bent my eyes in the shadows;
how I held myself down just to prove my love.

Now you want to offer elegies,
star-filled skies of forgiveness with a band of roses
but all you'll get from me is a cloud of smoke
nothing more than ash from a cigarette.

Published: Some Voices Sing, An International Anthology of Hope, produced by Blue Catharsis Publishing. It is available from Bookscrown: https://bookscrown.com/some-voices-sing-anthology-of-hope

Eating Marigolds…

I never thought I would love you so long
or that the peacocks would stop dancing
or that it would quit raining;
however, here I am waiting for flowers to grow on rooftops
competing with blackbirds
on my knees
hoping the Mother of God
will hear my prayers
as I whisper the rosary from page 37.
Someone below is smoking
clove cigarettes (so out of fashion)
and I am thinking of the young couple in Starbucks
snapping selfies, licking each other's fingers,
sharing earbuds
listening to 80's music,
dizzy on a love that's never been crucified
and I want to light the night
on fire for you.

Published in IMPRESSIONS & EXPRESSIONS Anthology of Contemporary Poetry,
Edited by Amita J. Sanghavi, ISBN: 9798515156084 July 2021

Now I Believe You

From my backyard, I look up into the night sky.

I see our ancient romance held together

by a cluster of stars:

bruised, broken and hardly noticeable

they blink in silence,

like unanswered messages taken for granted.

I look for more than mythical ruins,

more than 17 syllables to describe my feelings -

something beyond paranoia or nostalgia.

The confusion of love mixed with fear,

as if you promised to reveal a part of yourself

every time I walked away.

You said: "Whether you love someone for six days,

six weeks, six years or sixty -

you only love them once on repeat."

SUNKISSED WOMAN

I would give you a sun kissed woman
and a sand-colored day

except summer in my sky
is a loss of control
an opportunity to ask the body
what it remembers:

a taste that strips the mouth
of all recognition
a kiss more tangible
than the jolt of whiskey
and like elephants on a rampage
opening a wound

a falcon flies above
the tallest tree

I bleed

Clouds

High above my ordinary life
the sky is a witness.

The moment is average
& the thought of you
is a cloud passing through.

All I can come up with
to explain my lack luster attitude
is a word like bewilderment.

I too ask myself
why I bought the story of us,

something random,
ultimately unknowable,

kind of like a poetry book
I carried home
one night
holding it to my heart
because I thought it held
the promise
of transformation
and destiny

only to find the pages
were blank
even in the day light.

The Way I Love is a Liability

It's a crown of thorns,
a beating of cat tails and iron.

It rips flesh from my bones
tears my veins out
until I'm raw.

I prowl in black nights,
sleepless and wild haired,
hot from the heat earth releases
after she's held death's stare
longer than desire.

My love is burned,
crushed, mauled, exiled
impaled, stoned to death
and castrated.

People get used to the slaughter;
it's glued onto billboards,
sparks off pixelated surfaces.

Speaking loudly -
it isn't rape, it is roses!

The lines of my heart bleed out
and resurrect 12th century lovers.

A flawed story, a romance
of Godly proportions:
a set of Biblical translations

scar of tattoos, muted screams
carved from the inside out.

Acid Love

The taste of you on my tongue
is caustic.

You think I won't survive.

But you don't know about flowers
that grow from a sardonic earth:

African Violet, Azalea,
Amaryllis and lovely Gardenia.

I have blossomed through
droughts and hell.

It's your turn to fight
against dying.

Strings

Shall I give up on the soul mate

and suppose there are no great loves

except the quiet warmth of a steady commitment;

that holy matrimony of two

who meet in the grocery store on a Tuesday over grapes and pears?

Do they suddenly look up and lock eyes

or just bump into each other while leaning in to get a bag?

Maybe they meet in the airport,

talk about lost luggage and delayed flights

before they exchange email addresses.

I guess it doesn't really matter if they leave someone

to marry each other

or give up the cat and job to travel across country

for that simple meeting of two people

in an ordinary way, nothing at all like the movies.

I suppose it should not matter if they desert

that International hot date

who was just looking for a translator

because I assume in every language someone has gone to bed

asking themselves while staring at a blank ceiling

if a soul mate still exists for them.

I imagine someone is dreaming like I am,

that there is match for me -

and the Chinese saying about two souls being connected

by a string is true.

Sand Worship

Barefoot and shirtless, you stood tall
blocking the sun,
cigarette between ring finger
and middle finger
you said....

"I want idolatry. That's all.
Not mythologies or mirages.
Just solid gold worship."

Young. We laughed.

In the name of Jesus.
In the name of Billy Idol and Madonna.
In the name of fallen kings and moon goddesses.

And, now I sit alone on the beach
thinking of Isis and Osiris
wondering if you'll return
to be my light.

You promised.

Alone with Confessions

You write cello music
in blood
and lock ravaged beasts
away in the farthest recesses
of your mind...

in the same places where you confess
that it's impossible to free
yourself from Judah's screams
and Christ's betrayal.

I hear the holy angelic voices
singing in darkness.
I see your face heavy with ash
lines drawn from sacraments
and things unforgiven.

I cannot withdraw my hand
from the prophecy
when you've woven all of my stars
under your breastbone
and the air we share is filled
with that same light.

Keep breathing
and I'll find the path
to your heart.

Forest Fire

I wanted to fit into a Bible verse
clear as gin
distant as starlight
and leave no stronger presence
than mist on the lake
nothing greater than darkness itself
hiding the buck
shaving the velvet off new antlers
against tree bark.

I smuggled the crescent moon
under my shirt
until someone dropped
a lipstick rimmed
cigarette in the forest
and now I am to blame.

Sunflower Tattoos

When I look into the fields
I see the ghost of you
a pale version, a faded view
drifting into the yellow fractals
of painted stories left behind
now somehow falling open
as you turn to face me.
I catch each petal in my hand
except there are too many,
they are too large.
The power of loving you
overwhelms me as lost years
of sweat stained labor:
flesh torn from the bone, bleeding,
yet brilliant and common
as the sun on my skin.

Love's Sanctuary...

You arrived in a dream
   and left the same way.

Part of me thought it was overblown
how you might just touch me
in one minute to change life as I knew it
and walk like a flower
among the thorns of my discolored heart.

The other part of me knew
it was you
   would always be you

to rise like a sweet fragrance
in the strangely lonesome field

I call *myself*

and populate it with love.

Just when I start to think it is dead
and dried up and gone

with the memories uprooted
and nothing to show for it

except a few seeds...

suddenly the selfless joy of our embrace
opens like a rose in sunlight.

Once again

   I am surrounded by our flowers

      in full bloom.

My Body: A Mermaid Graveyard

You arrived as a sluice of dark waters
cutting across my leg.

You died twice. First in my sleep.
Your little seahorse face floated up to mine:

small unformed mermaid lips,
a tiny dream that drifted back into the sea.

I never knew that I was also an ocean
until you lived inside of me. And, decided to leave.

I had a name selected for you: White Sky.
I misunderstood. You never wanted to live in a body.

Survivalist

I knew a man
stealth as a hunter
cold as winter
and he could float in water
for days
like the dead
or a hungry polar bear
on a block of ice
his nose in the air
on the prowl
for the languid seal
who gives, and gives,
then gives it all she has got,
until blood
spills from her skin
and the wishbone breaks
in half.

Haunted Waters

It is not the balloons or red umbrellas
or how I made a ziggurat out of myself
weaving spiderwebs thru my ribs.

I cannot expect an origami boat
to float around the globe
and arrive as a seraphic message.

My blue phantoms are hawk-eyed
even though they are fabricated
and henna tattoos look good on them.

Their pale ink fades in the rain.
The smell is not death, it is stale wine
broken eggs and wet grass.

They focus on what I have lost:
patterned wall paper, you, miniature operas
and the asylum my memories claim.

My prayers end up mummified,
brightly painted creatures on the sea floor
without a voice or higher self.

In that world there is an anchor,
a shipwreck, and curious translucent entities
who mimics the stars:

Drunk poets, spurned lovers, depressed mothers
misdiagnosed schizophrenics, dissociated identities
diving into the mouth of melancholy.

Teeth and claws fill the waters a purplish black
as if someone told them a sacrifice thicker than
water was expected before sunrise.

As for me, I am here waiting for you
to break the surface from twilight's imagination
and emerge as the light of resurrection.

SIPHONED LIGHT

I went in search of dead poets
who have skin like arsenic,
chipped fingernails,
tiny feet that will not carry them far

and bones made of coal
with sulfur lips stretched across filed teeth
not required to bleed
or grow life

they curl legs around legs
listen for pennies
tossed into fountains
brass oracles just waiting to splash

prophecies or curses
spun as webs across barren ribs
woven in Fallopian tubes
unlacing the song

I keep trying to memorize
with my eyes closed
counting off white stanzas
as fabrics unravel

a ghost over my naked shoulder
who resembles you
a mirage in the mirror
reaching for my throat

but no, it is not your light
I carry, it is my fire,
it is not your song, I sing, it is mine,
be gone witch, be gone.

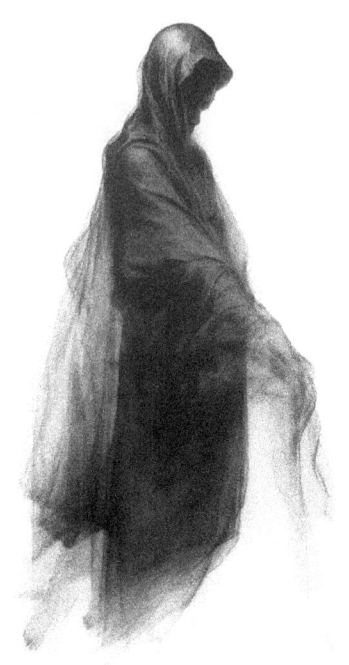

Forbidden City

You will not find a map to the city
buried deep in my heart.

I will not give you directions
or show you how to illuminate that path.

There is nothing you can give or take
from the essence of me.

I will not open the secret chambers
for your vulgarity or burning demands.

Pure Love is the one guide you need
and the only way you will ever discover me

Taking Back the Words

I keep trying to write a poem where I take back all the things
I should have never said.

It is not working.

The list is too long. The reasons are too many.
The memories thaw and puddle into a ring at the bottom of a glass.

Then the coyotes start howling...
it is useless, it's foolish and it's always too late.

I cannot help but wonder why?
Why we do these things to each other?

We know better.
And, yet we continue to use our tongues
like knives.

This time I was not the one who said stupid, mean
and dumb ass things.

It is just that your hideous words reminded me
of the horrible times I did.

And, the sad truth is those unkind things
erase the beauty,

so sometimes cliches are all we have.

The Stuff Indie Films are Made of

In that frame, we were never the same.

That's the best place I can think of to start a poem
because now you can fill in the images
between everything that ends and begins again.

Your long silence. Decades. Smothered.

I tried to use the metaphors of popular images:
smoke, lip stick stained cigarettes, red stilettos
and the stuff indie films are made of.

My eyes could be peeled out. My mouth taken off.

I experimented with the idea of jazz saxophones,
burlesque dancers and bathtub gin -
speak easy and the secret narratives of lovers.

Our half-truths were never so subtle or sexy.

Then I found your photo of the black birds,
gray clouds with ghost like limbs and trees tangled.
Whose heart is in that sky? Who is nailed to the tree?

There are birds outside the frame eating these precious things.

The Blue Buddha Painting

The blue Buddha painting
knifed to shreds
on Naylor Street, San Francisco
is unearthed from the depths of her mind
twenty years later
while she walks on Painted Feather Drive.
It is in the winds,
bruised like the bones of an ancestor
left to rot with stiff knees
in red clay. The orange
mango sunset howls, a solar flare,
a puzzle solved
in this cellophane wrapped history
where two broken people once entertained the idea
of marriage at Taj Mahal,
and it pierces her thoughts
as she realizes the blade
was meant for her.

In the Shadow of a Hunter's Moon

October has passed and left me with the emblem
of your mouth on mine.

A monogram of magical phenomena,
shape-shifting, sparrow in the hand.

An irreverent radiance satiated, overflowing;
suffused with autumn's pigments.

Yesterday the world was thirst and day dream.
Today it's full of sequestered aspirations.

I am here. The muted song no less eloquent.

The ghost of your hand on my hip, taciturnity
in your eyes, a reflection of morning.

It carries the solemn weight of silence
except for the first rain of November.

Don't Send Flowers, Send Dostoevsky

Read the words close to my skin
so, I can translate the heat
of your breath -
I want to feel when the murder
is near.

I want to hear your confession:
tell me you believe love survives
without provocation
without your permission -
unexpected, unexplainable
as a riddle:
a string between two people
that may become tangled and far apart
but never lost.

Tell me again about punishment,
leave no word unspoken.
What page starts to bleed in the snow,
scream in suffering?
Please don't skip the passage of God.
Whisper it into my breast bone
graceful as one who drank too much Vodka
the night before.

Remember we are not the lucky ones,
death is not coming for us
anytime soon
and this body is capable of both wicked
and unspeakable things...
it's a dungeon of confusion
a prison filled with horrors and shame.

I only feel free
when you speak fire into me
when your tongue leaves
a trail of flames.

It was lover's kismet
that held the pages of our book
in one place;
that brought you back to me
scared, ravaged, and thin
holing my soul.

My Intricate Hallucination

I went in search of you
trolling through a past that I created.
One that never actually
existed
except in the reverie
I built
in my heart:
a castle of laughter
from a strand of licorice,
imagining you
to be
someone
that you never were
never will
be.

In the Afterglow

We fast forward thru random images
bypass the bodyguard of stories
turn off the sound and
subtitles, so we can leave
long and short vowels,
skipping to how the end begins
where lips are locked
on lips, hips against hips
and how magnificent the afterglow is
thru filters, tilted
where the strangest hauntings
from the bad girls' club
are written into the script
without oxygen
as someone laughs in the background
earth bound with a heart full of prisoners
not searching for anything
not bleeding for anyone
just reaching for a glass of wine
feeling as iconic as false gods
with bone tattoos
in smut novels
not willing to admit desire
is a sleeping giant
or how the loss that occurred in episode 7
was an afterthought
that covered the garden in ashes
an left gaping exit wounds
because it's the price that's extracted
for confronting demons
for stealing fire.

Telepathy

I know you are hoping for a telegraph
or a sign of telepathy.

Anything to confirm you exist in my story
in the cross wires of memory.

I remember:

an eclipse, a hurricane and a political
catastrophe that pales by comparison.

If we experience life thru more than a body,
thru more than the earth and stars...

and know that we each carry a scar,
the influence of a shattered cosmos.

Love is not an inevitable word, it is not
even sublime, but it is what I have got.

Angels glow in flight, hold mystery
and carry constellations of prayer within.

Last night I dreamt of you, it was easy.
You said something about forgiveness.

It felt real and I did not want to wake up.
I have stopped looking for you in this world.

You are a lot like a holiday:

full of sparkle, expensive expectations
and shimmy glitz
that sash-shay around the house
boasting
about a wide range of surprises.

Then there is the interlude
diva speeches, fine wines, fancy cars
big business and treats.

So, let's get this straight,
I am a woman made from slate and iron
a string of lights won't change that.

When Sundays were all we had...

we pretended it was the rest of our lives
as we laid in the sunlit yard
mad with ideas, sexy in velvet kisses
sipping cocktails with stately names like Texas Tea
eating egg salad sandwiches
preaching the Gospel of Matthew, Mark, Luke and John
while the world fought wars miles away
the bees built a hive in the oak tree
and when the praying mantis landed on my leg
I took it as a sign:
our love was the savior.

The boundary line...

The boundary line
stretches along the highway

to divide and shield us
from wayward tendencies:

our racing emotions
that might otherwise
spin out of control
and careen
into one another.

It is after all a matter of life
and death...

our hearts are buckled in tight
behind glass,
surrounded with iron and metal,

all that protective air.
Beware of twilight
it is the most dangerous
time of day
when the light reflects
off the words

we mouth to one another
silently in passing.

Misplaced Apostrophe

You leap through me like a tiger

and insist on absence

from the abstract miseries created

by divorce -

similar to the end of flesh

which seems to appear suddenly,

even though we know

one day everyone's breath

escapes finally

like a 1,000 misspelled words

left blue in the cold

and translated incorrectly.

Smugglers

tonight I plan to smuggle
the fragrance
of love
across the borders
of your dreams
and break through
that wire fence
intended to keep
me out

I Wrote a Prayer for You

I wrote a prayer for you:
a color between violet and green
with all the hope I had
and it was no more dangerous
than a field mouse.

In response you claimed
generosity was not a good substitute
for an apology -
so, I choose to be mute.

I added a little more brandy
to my eggnog
and you stormed off searching for clues,
amassing torn memories:
cloudy skies, wild horses, and circling hawks.

Meanwhile the book of God
has not changed:
swollen, turbulent, raging,
punitive, prophetic
and no one of credence dares to
admit mistakes.

Perhaps my song to you
was juvenile -
a little too nude in my bare feet
and I should take back
every word,
an array of discarded clothes
on the floor.

Maybe I will dress in ashes,
go gather speckled eggs,
pigeons, melon rinds, orange peels
and create spiced wine
to cure the righteousness festering
in your belly.

Or I can stand around in a dimly lit kitchen
licking the brandy
and sugar off my fingertips
staring at my reflection
in the dark
conversing with wind chimes.

And, you can keep yourself locked
inside a narrative
where you are blameless
as the chimera in your fractured mind:
a spirit animal
with a pocket full of hashtags
and Sunday selfies.

Suicidal Planets

Momentarily I embellish the beauty
of our union:

dancing to a jazz howling sax,
fever and pitch,
and a flare of our laughter rockets across the sky
to become in one breath
a blaze of discord
somewhere in a vast distance what was "our future."

Not unlike a meteor shower
but not the same either.

I cannot say if I imagined the constellation
of us
only that I remember we loved
without heliographs
and maybe that is why we lost
one another

in the dark bedlam,
as if turmoil was an afterthought,
a lawlessness of its own,

a nebulous place between taste
and yearning.

We Want to Be Taken by Surprise

We want it to be pleasant
and as sexy bottle of vanilla vodka,
cool as a silk blouse
against the skin of mid-life
and to draw no logical conclusions
about the edge
between lust and love.

If it can't be as swift as a bird
defying the sky
or a tiger sinking its teeth
into the helpless neck
of a wounded other,
then we will settle for dirty martinis,
slurp a drinkable mud
and drown in tart filled sludge.

For at least the symbols will blend
and fade easily
as a distant dream
while we disappear below our equator
knowing
that we had everything to do
with this charade.

The Light in Your Eyes

The only star
I see
is the light
in your eyes
while you tell me
about how hard it is
to discover
heaven
in a world
of nightmares,
black skies
& worm
holes.

Forgotten Ancestors

In ochre sunlight reflected on the curved backs of horses
running along the line of charcoal pigments
deep in the cragged rocks of France on a cave wall
I hear there are bull shapes painted
with black horns and rectangular faces
I hear there are lions without manes,
and constellations that guide shamans
and altars made from stones;
that those same ancestors built massive sundials
elaborate gateways to worship Mother Earth.
It turns out to be one large rustic sacred cathedral
with ancestral inspired creatures
dancing bison, racing rustic beasts;
that call to us in our dreams
century after century from cave walls
and we rise from our blurry narrow slumber
to embrace the oxygen deprived vision
and wander again into the passageway
of art to return to creation's womb.

Spilling

The ink of your words
spread into my mute heart
and left a stain.

Failed Seeds

I am not sure about where it goes
when it goes
only that I know the time for loving you is over
and it resides somewhere
below light
as the entombed myth.

What I remember must be fiction
because oddly
I am not burning at both ends
to explain,
hold onto the story
or even keep myself from the underbelly
of bitterness.

The echo of your breath and outline
of your body next to mine
becomes rigid,
disappears from my dreams;
smears on paper
the same as a character who dies
unexpectedly early
and leaves the audience
buried in silence.

Fading news of your life,
how you married into a suitable Greek tragedy
or cut corners to get needs met,
reminds me of nothing
except empty backyards with dried lawns
suffocated by weeds
and a ceremony of dead flowers:

a series of failed seeds
planted many moons ago.

Encounter

After being unwanted

for so long

he walked toward me

silent as the sun

ready to ignite

a matchbox of soul

and it felt like

foreplay to me.

Ensconce

our love story is unrecognizable
filled with pockmarks

perpetual tide pools
undone by the wild possessive sea

determined to revoke the taste of you
and to steal the shape of your body

in its place there is broken glass
seaweed, bone fragments

someone tell the sea sorceress
to put away the pitch fork, she is too late

I have already invented new names
for what I have saved

Schizophrenic Swerve

Today the voices are quiet
and the ghosts have gone underground.

For a moment, I can rest one eye
(the darker one)
while the sky opens its curtains
like a witch's skirt
copious enough to seduce
my fears
but not enough to stop
the trolley
of thoughts from skidding
off the rails.

Not Equal to the Gods

I didn't know a man could turn sour
or flame could go flat
until I watched the sun slip off his lips
and fall like ice
back-washed into Bourbon.

I had no clue that my body
would give away the stories I hoped to hide
or that my heart would saunter
into a dark place,
coil up like a sleeping cat.

I remember how he spoke
as if he alone knew the secret of sound;
knew the mystery of flowers
and my name.

Only a shadow lingers
against the wall,
curses and footprints,
when all I wanted was a love poem.

Everlasting

Like the renovation of love
in a ruined past
there are some things that should happen only once.

And, if I caused you to believe
that we could outrun our shadows
or the long good-bye we never actually said
as we stretched time across years,
then I am the fool.

As for you,
you are the light I live for.

For the Love of Oranges

My lover, well one of them anyway,
read several poems to me, two at night,
and sometimes three during the day,
mixed with the heat of whiskey in between.

Later after we broke up, he complained
that I did not pay attention to his voice,
failed to notice the inflections and pitch
of his numb tongue, heavy with emphasis.

I thought I had. I thought I was pretty good.
I ran my fingers through his hair cooing
at all the important stanzas and haiku.
I chirped mating calls in return to his.

Until today. A guy with a sleepy look on his face
selling oranges out of the back of his trunk
caught my attention with his gentle voice saying:
"Sweet lady, oranges, sweet, sweet oranges over here."

Lifeboat

The secret of bliss is to enter it
again and again...

to infiltrate it without worrying about drowning
or a deceptive ending,
or if your lover will stay on the shore
smoking cigarettes, staring at their phone
as you float on
searching for joy in sad places;
while you sail beyond
the horizon
simply because it sent out an invitation
soliciting the uncharted:

a midnight swim and the untold
story of you.

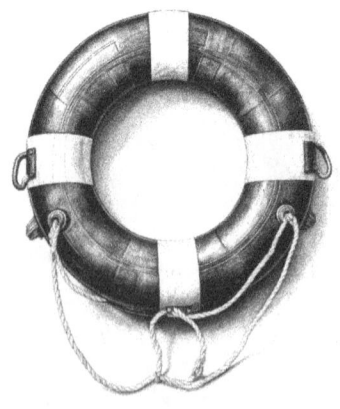

Vanquished

From the beginning,
everything was used against me
like a radioactive nightmare
blistering my soul
until something quit growing
inside of me.

It is true, I was afraid
of falling, of not belonging.

I was unable to resist the break,
unwilling to hesitate
or catch myself
from being nothing more
or less
than a wound
that fades into silence.

blue lanterns in midsummer

- for Darcy

your body coiled and pale
the same as a tropical flower
laced with alkaloids
scorched in the sun without protection

a poem betwixt:
wagging tongues and prophecy
imploring God for answers
declaring we are not
made from bone, flesh or dirt

the skin peels:
cells, micro chemicals, vapors
exposed clavicles
hip bones hostage to the blue
take over of silence

nothing evolved here:
except your words that continue to bloom
from your belly
all the children not born
who refuse to rest
in the salt
of a coffee stained earth

upspoken earth
drawn in the shape of a heart
on your shirt
the same color as your eyes
where you now dream
without us

Muses

Most all of them are surrounded with blue air
nearly naked, surely nude
under a thin veneer of glazed hues
as they stretch long past their shadows;
quite similar to a cat, almost
like smoke
they linger with the moon
swallow flowers, eat gardenias
and disappear as easily.

They are bad tempered, inconsiderate,
mistaken for the Magdalena
or a woman who looks nothing like her
with a jeweled clip in her hair
almost regal
lips with a dash of red,
wrapped up in linens of gold
and unrequited love.

Some of them are married
and painted 27 times in oil only to desire
lemonade, faraway places
while others are wooed with chalk,
with doves on walls,
desired for that perfect neck -
elongated, elegant, cubist
and some save the artist from insanity
while others take pleasure
in driving it in, driving it deep
into chaos,
that creative madness.

In the Spirit of Ezra Pound

A chilling sorcery
painted with stunning precision
and a single man
determined to know what could not be lost;
what could be saved
in translation.

Women had grey eyes
or no eyes. Their limbs twisted
around other limbs. Green
sofas in empty rooms
without musical sequence,
mere metronomes -
abstract art; the cluttered horrors
of what was to come
and 100 hundred belly aches
void of love.

Against the backdrop
of violence, a framed annihilation
of intelligence,
the death
of a flower, or just your soul
and the realization
you are more like a lithograph
signed in pencil
than the center of anything
important.

One Soul

In the heart of my heart
stands the naked
radiance of you
in Love
like the inner knowing
of God
conscious of only one
Soul
divided by two.

Tobacco

Here I am the cash crop
ready to be used

as a recreational drug
the essence

of consumption
in your mouth,

a slow thrill
between your lip and tongue.

I am everything
I have always been

cultivated, transplanted
rolled, stored and cured
for the stories of shamans,
lovers and every man.

Until you find me,
ready for the bargain

like a prayer
in the small hours of night

turned into a gift
that rises toward heaven.

You Are My Earth

Your body
   slips
through my fingertips
and I touch
the wet firmness
  of you -
made of water
and earth
you cannot resist
my caress until at last
all you crave
    is
this embrace.

Cineastas

We exist in the shadows
left behind;
meanwhile you imagine I've
forgotten, or misplaced the image
of two particles of light
recorded in digital spaces
we never speak of.

I hear our voices
declare a new found territory
as our eyelids flicker
in black and white
our hearts suspended
in gray space
floating in rewind.

Leave the Lamp On

We are uncomfortably close
for being so far apart.

I dream about you
relaxed in semi-darkness
with feline eyes
and a ring of smoke
rising from your inflated lips.

Except you've probably given that up
for a trendy flair -
juice fasting and moving meditations;
maybe yoga,
and snacking on raw leafy things
like the holy kale.

But in the lamplight of my reverie
we talk all night
without fear or worry
about the autopsy of words
or the brutal
dismemberment of ego.

I don't know if it is sad or not,
or if it matters,
that once I saw a rainbow
shine through you
and pass a band of color into me
like a night bird
through the darkest part of sky.

I was sure you were good for it.

San Francisco Jangle

It is rush hour, so we move quickly
we are the sound of noise
big as an elephant we sway
in a city made of ruckus and riot
shaped by the Gold Rush and Barbary Coast
ruthless and full of sentiment
laced with arsenic
we gather at stop lights
pigeons fight over scraps of food at our feet
as a pandemonium gathers itself
in our bones:
other people's thoughts become our own
unspoken they hover in the air
then drop, now lost among the garbage in the gutter.
It is not so hard to rise above it though.
It is all about who you know
in this sophisticated hullabaloo,
especially if you're willing to
get confetti in your hair
wear strapless gowns, champagne stained
in an avant-garde twist or two
and dance on the skyline.

Thirst

He is a man
Made from books
Walking with loose change
In his pockets
Like some kind of Messiah
Hoping for a miracle
Who wants a one
More than the myth
He arrives on my page
Ready to drink the water
From my skin
Like a fish too long out of water
Ready to dive in
Beyond what is desired
Into what simply is
As he licks the salt from my hips

Becoming a Falcon

After years of reading Dante
and Virgil's poetry
I made a choice not wear their words
or to be in your Odyssey.
I stopped dressing in your flower narratives
woven from hippie-boho gardens
that led to zigzagged paths filled with mosquitos
and worm bottomed tequila.
I gave it up and
my heart was speared on a spike
burned, charred and returned to me again
the same way all stolen things are -
as if one should be grateful
for the malfeasance.
I said goodbye to the tapestries, tables, plates,
houses, artwork, wine and languages of the gods.
It was counterfeit!
I traded it for something solvent
and gave myself wings.

Alabaster

I wanted to write about white, because it has a clean slate.
I've spilled milk and witnessed the robes
of holy people; been inside the edges of cathedrals
and heard the death message a pure lily brings.
I've worn wedding dresses. Stood in the shadow
of Greek Gods; been to baptisms and fell, bled in the snow.
I remember the broken alabaster box from a Biblical passage,
the fragrance poured onto the feet of a rejected Messiah.
It's the tint of outcasts and sinners...
The color of angel wings after the monsoons.
and if I stand a little straighter
maybe I will grow some.

Dreamcatcher

I am walking on black horizons
in semi-moonlight with a fish kite
lulled by the breeze of memories
towards a distant home
past peach trees, over ripe,
when I hear your call from a faraway place
like a coyote
and the swans fly from the blue lake
before I can say
this is why I enter the dream
because I know you will find me
and I will move blindly
towards your voice
thru tulip fields
into an opaque night
where with one touch
you change the atmosphere
and water flows
from a stone.

Lotus in the Mud

I walked in darkness
my skin torn from the root
open without a boundary.
I was transparent
and convinced that if you came close
with mantras, holy chants, and musical prayers
it would cause the gates
of my heart to open
because the empire of your compassion
is as extravagant as a goddess
on a tiger
bejeweled in forgotten wonder
and I am hungry
for sutras -
starving for the embrace
that only comes
from the light within.

Published in IMPRESSIONS & EXPRESSIONS Anthology of Contemporary Poetry, Edited by Amita J. Sanghavi, ISBN: 9798515156084 July 2021

The Grace Surrounding Us

You told me to be like a jacaranda tree
in the moon valley.

From the fall of petals, I cannot escape.
From the crushed, torn skin against stone, there is no relief.

The dead clutch at the living;
their greed for what they did not finish hangs onto us.

I am near the deceased. I hear the trembling.
The night is stripped of moss and bark.

You told me to be like small animals in the forest
who drink by dark blue waters, distant.

This is where I remember your name
and discover the swollen rim of your ancestors' eyelids.

You beckon for me to cover myself, to say goodbye
to the sunlight that entitles, burns and blinds.

Your song, the one written for you before you were born
is in the background. The angels have arrived.

You ask me to be like the lavender petals fallen to the ground
and surrender to the grace surrounding us.

Published in DEMO GOG International Magazine, Internet and Print, October 2022

The Journey to Love

All the folktales of my life
Brought me here
To the bridge of our story
At the edge of light
And shadow's beauty
Where your mouth on my mouth
Is the taste that tempts me
Towards the beginning
Of your skin on mine
Of your fire burning into my body
Like two mirrors
Bright with the open revelation
That arrives after
Drinking the tears of a lover
Swallowing
The fruit of an everlasting
Tenderness spoken
Naked, raw skin to skin
While making love all night

A love story inside structure of color

you said, indigo is for soul love
blue is for the upper room

yellow is saved for those bent shoulders
who need to cry
but red, red is only for the same person
over time who carries the mouth of flowers
with the kiss of promise but not sobriety
easily lost somehow in the ivory of creation

like a work of art or a secret bargain
formed with our eyes half closed
where we long for the color of truth
and this love in the soft green of willows

Published in Flax to Gold, Kreative South Africa, 2007

Fourth Chamber of My Heart

I used to go on long drives
seeking life's meaning.

I found there were more words
for head than heart in society,
so I took to reading
palms.

Misfortune, destiny, and a universe
of love in the open hand, circle
creases of thumb where the wounded
child lives.

Unsatisfied. My desire took me
into a book of nights. I lost sight.
I gave up everything material
to dissolve in sand.

I should know better than the tarot
or searching heaven in quiz
of zodiac redemption.

Don't blame me for dreams
living on possibility, swallowing
shapeless air.

I do not know how to map arteries
or veins between intellect and consequence
of emotional strays.

It doesn't stop the innermost
of what I fear or anything
I feel.

I should have road signs of predictability
that point to the heart in duty,
complete with directions.

I am conditioned
by impairment of social function,
so I tour my journey
in great sorrow.

My love did not die.
I simply covered the tracks
to offer no way back.

If there were a road less travelled
then I suppose it is the one
carved inside of me
I let no one
follow.

Tears of a Pilgrim Poet: Sparrow

I volunteered to be a house of water
to the dry bones of a pilgrim poet.

I picked him up at the train station
with his dark hat turned sideways.

He said his blood was thin and he was tired,
but sitting together was a cure.

I surrendered my prayers and good merit
for lakes of suffering that shone in his eyes.

I witnessed the vines circling around his mind
and triangles of mysticism on his neck.

He gathered the fragments of himself
as a smoking rose wishing to bloom again

in his heart – hoping to grow large enough
to nurture the songs inside.

We sat on a rock by the ocean
ignoring the gray clouds gathering north.

He opened a notebook of songs he wrote on a bus,
and pulled out a wood carving of lovers.

Explaining that one holds the other, just exactly so,
no matter which way it is rotated.

He started to sing about just walking off shore,
right into the sea forever translucent -

about lovers, the zodiac, and broken shells
about saints, and people with sad eyes.

I realized then we have no idea who anyone is
and it might be true true we entertain angels unaware.

I did not expect him to carry off my heart.
Or to give me his.

Somehow
that is exactly what he did.
It doesn't stop the innermost
of what I fear or anything
I feel.

I should have road signs of predictability
that point to the heart in duty,
complete with directions.

I am conditioned
by impairment of social function,
so I tour my journey
in great sorrow.

My love did not die.
I simply covered the tracks
to offer no way back.

If there were a road less travelled
then I suppose it is the one
carved inside of me
I let no one
follow.

Soul Means Bird

On a torn sofa in a dimly lit living room
you sing about the weightlessness of wind -
how tiny the world is from that perspective.

I consider turning up the lights
offering popcorn, beer, or something like cake.
Instead, I lean in the hallway.

I wonder if the company you keep shapes you
or if the places you choose
are more like birdhouses on a porch?

Are you more sensitive to movement -
did you learn to read faces and palms?
Do you miss the people you leave behind?

The image of a big sky enters my mind
and I think you have flown too close
to the gap between living and dying.

I decide to make my presence known
flick on the switch, shuffle in my slippers
heavy with psychology and analysis.

Then you turn to me singing
the blues are not my home, you are
and this is where I want to, I land.

Our Lady of Sorrows

I prefer the petite chapel
reserved for Our Lady of Sorrows

where in my solitude

I can listen to the silence
and light a small candle

I can offer the gift of remembering
to honor the journey that brought me here

as I kneel in the early morning
darkness

among the fragrance of flowers
and old wood

I can offer gratitude for the light
that shines from the angels

to eliminate the pain
in my heart

I would be lost
except for the beauty of grace

I might not live
except for this love

I might not feel
so alive, so transformed

Our Hearts Are Listening

We hear the voices of mother earth
And father sky
The cries of unborn children
The whale song
And the cries of those we've lost
We hear the voices of wild creatures
Torn from the womb of life
We hear them both far and wide
From the beginning of time

We are listening to souls
As they arrive thru heavens gates
The sound of Pleiades
And the stories from double fish
Held together by the string as the
Stars murmur their iridescent light
Whispering to us of other worldly
Guides. We hear you: dragon, werewolf, satyr, and unicorn.

We hear the drumbeat of holy light
As lions cross the threshold
Of a new era and reclaim sacred territory. So we too enter our hearts
In full pandemonium of animal lore
And embrace the meaningful
Our totems: giraffe, white bear, wolf, wild dog, lion, turtle and frog.
Bold, courageous, loyal, resourceful
And gracious
We release the eagle, the falcon, owl and raven
Thankful for their power

We open the vortex of our hearts
On the burnt edge of red rocks
To fly across the rainbow
And soar into crystal blue sky
Euphoric with possibility
As we burn hot on fire
In the sun
Like children in love

Naming the Cherry

She told me it was *horrible*,
a lethal hurricane rained night and day
starting the clock toward my birth.

I went seven days without a name.
Certain I would be a boy they did not mind
scar on my cheek, forceps
under my eye from force, pulling me
into life with a scream.

She said they knocked her out cold
and it was a good thing
since it was the hottest tropical summer
in years.

They were all very worried
about the orchards,
my grandfather's heart,
and how the oranges need rain -

   except she craved cherries,
       already out of season.

When They Were Seventeen

If it wasn't for the motorcycle breaking down
on a hot Florida night in 1966
or for the barn party,
then I would not have been conceived.

If they weren't in the middle of superstition
or on the edge of an inexact darkness,
they might have grown to love one another
before they were forced to marry.

But as it was, he came too soon,
and she really doesn't remember the details
except they were akimbo and clammy
with bad breath; lost in the fear of what might
crawl up between her legs.

Unabbreviated

Maybe leaving home really is the beginning of freedom.
I don't know. That's just what he keeps telling me.
Like immunity is found sleeping on a park bench
painted forest green
as if everyone could be forgiven;
considered good enough
even after they've been discarded
the same as day old bread
from Whole Foods.
Perhaps he is right.
I want to believe there is less cruelty in world
and it is found hiding
where the dirty kids spange for change -
the willfully homeless
who crash on sidewalks
in a messy state of affairs
and collect citations for loitering,
for flashing cardboard signs
that read "smile."
And, then there is the reality of it,
as if it is the worst thing
to live feral in the streets,
to trek across the states hitchhiking
off the kindness of strangers in blind faith.
I realize then it doesn't matter
what I declare or exclude
there are people bigger than me
in this little place
I call home.

Published in IMPRESSIONS & EXPRESSIONS Anthology of Contemporary Poetry, Edited by Amita J. Sanghavi, ISBN: 9798515156084 July 2021

Gutter Punk

I look for you in accidental places
in between golds and blacks.
I expect to see you among the travelers
together in a hovel:
a sidewalk caravan of backpacks,
out of tune guitars, drift-less expressions.
My blood is in your veins
as you tramp, hobo, hitchhike across America;
some spit on you, you roll in beer...
some feed, house and try to rescue.
They're looking for me inside of you.
What kind of mother? Who did this to you?
You do not listen, do not care.
I bend myself in half,
then again, fold another corner of my heart
until I am an origami version of myself.
I wait for hope to reappear,
my face pressed into the Earth.

Street Monk

he is out on the streets again
   leaving behind everyone he knows
   in scandal or just to be away

   with a guitar and duffel bag
   pounding bus stops ready to start over
   anywhere will do
   just so long as it does not sound like old times
   or somewhere he has already been

   he can drink his own season of darkness
   without any help
   and give God a handshake
   without asking for favors or free clothes

   he has already turned down dozens of free blows
   with their skirts hiked up high in chill of night
   but he prefers the slow motion of morphine women
   to the bigoted philosophies waiting in bushes

   he is on the streets again
   ready to sell valuables
   just so long as no one will ask him
   answers to questions he wants to forget
   because he would rather die alone
   in a strange city
   than explain anything to this world
   with all her final demands
   and taxations
   bitter practiced pricks of stealing breaths
   from inmates on death row

he will keep on walking the streets
accept the kindness of strangers
give up iconoclasts -
the bourgeois, obscenities, and blasphemies
because he can live on a mouthful of smoke

so, he will not hold his breath
waiting for life to apologize
for what is insane, mad, and cruel
since he is already crazy, he doesn't mind
if you think so too

A Study in Poppies

You eat the opium,
crush the red petals to your lips
and fall back upon pillows
as if Morpheus gave you the kiss of dreams.

I simply pray
this is not the painful stretch of fate
cursed to a young man
casually on the path of sugared skulls
sleeping in smoking dens
where souls burn on hot wires
and skin melts
down in a hiss of skeletal remains.

I remember you
as the champion of love
and a happy kid
with a twist of sweet innocence
always in conversation
with trees
before the pipe found its way
to your lips.

Nine Dragons

Born on a lucky day, I carry a paper lantern
and rice candy. We walk for hours
from China Town and to the Mission.

The morphine queen strolls through your veins,
turns your mouth slag and metallic –
locks you into a Chinese box,
so, it is impossible to learn you by heart.

You are my father but you are too young
to be my father, and like a lost art,
you do not recognize yourself.

We stop at City Lights to read a few books
and hide from the sun as it threatens to excavate
the vessel of your life.

I am five and already tired of sweet and sour,
animal years, incantations and premonitions.
I swallow pennies while the Rolling Stones echo
and Ginsberg is writing Howl.

The wind at 5th and Market chaps my lips
as the sundial of my childhood is shadowed
by your imminent death.

Another Word for "Mother"

The first time I heard it I was four. He slapped her hard on the face and she fell into the wall. She cried in the bathroom for a long time. Her mascara was still smeared when she set our plates for dinner. After she left for work, I asked him, "What does it mean? What is it?" He did not look at me while he cut into the rare meat on his dish or as his fork slid with a noise across his front teeth. But as it bled into a thin pool of flavor on the cracked plate, he looked straight into my eyes and replied, "Don't be stupid, just shut up and pass the salt."

Behind Door #9

In a one room hotel
   we sit cross leg on the floor
eating sardines straight from the can
   their heads and eyes swim.

This is no time to complain,
       it is 1971.

He is twenty-two, a military son.
   He pushes his shirt sleeves up,
tattooed heroin history on thin forearms.

I have never known him any other way.

His brown paper bag beer
   is sin passed in the space between us.
I take a sip,
   think I am equal.

I hope my mother will come back;
   she left us with a few things hanging in the closet.
He put a gun to her head
   one time too many.

It's in the nightstand,
   it's under the pillow,
   it's in his pocket.

He says:
"close your eyes Cherub."

It is a good day, so I tilt my head back
   squint my eyes, peek through my lashes.

In his shirt pocket is a gold foil square,
   a two penny liquor store find.
He unwraps it, tells me:
  "open your mouth."

I feel it on my tongue,
   it is sweet, it is warm, it melts quickly.
My hand covers chocolate sweet teeth.
   He smiles at me and winks.
He has purple circles under his eyes
   that I do not ask him to wash.

Late tonight when the fog rolls in,
  when it is blue dark,
a strange woman will come up
  from the streets with ratty hair
while I pretend to sleep
  in the corner, under the window
       on the floor;

while I pick the pink flowers off
  the rotting wall paper
       later.

Now the sun is out,
  it is clear day,
  it is my birthday.

I can count to four fingers...
   He is proud
       to be my father.

Hobo Cavalcade

You've made the train your metaphor.

Railway sounds in the distance,

metal to metal, box cars, muted freight colors,

cracked lips holding cigarettes,

muffled voices lost in eye watering winds.

You are there in a series of flickers,

a folded version of yourself passing quickly

through anonymous towns -

ash, gray, sepia with a touch of snow.

A blur of enlightenment I cannot hold.

I see the wide-eyed child in you

who creates a kingdom from his dreams

and I realize

when the phone rings

you are only as lost as you want to be.

Published in IMPRESSIONS & EXPRESSIONS Anthology of Contemporary Poetry, Edited by Amita J. Sanghavi, ISBN: 9798515156084 July 2021

For the Old Homeless Man

You, with the long white beard
and the ripped sleeping bag
over your shoulders,
reading a tattered book
(a title I can never seem to catch)
while you sit Zen style,
every morning
under the alcove of the Bay Bridge
on Folsom Street,
counting coins
that sparkle in a few feet of sunlight,
smoking second hand cigarettes
with lipstick
stuck to the filters.

I want you to know I see you.

I think of you when I go home at night.
I wonder what life you left behind
and if anyone cried
or if you simply walked away from unspeakable things
to disappear into the fog
and fading lines
of this poem.

Naked Man Smoking in the Alley

He's got that blue funk
look in his eye,
black grease for hair
and the stench of glum
rises like urine
to meet the gray San Francisco
afternoon, mid-day
outline of his downgraded heart
against the wall
next to the dumpster
like he found a business castle
rendered worthless
by his naked appearance
as he inhales
the spoils of dignity,
trafficked across borders
by shepherds,
sucks in the sacrifice of child brides,
while he leans sideways
with his pants around his ankles:
a crushed gangster
smoking the day dreams
of ghosts
like it's his last hope.

That Light Which Lights the Longer Light

I want to write a poem like you
full of coffee, the neighbor's barking dog,
left over pizza and popcorn.

That poem where you talk about Joni Mitchell,
finding God and
changing the clocks to match our idea of seasons.

Where you talk about how hot it was
the year I was born.
How that August Florida heat could kill a man -
imagine a pregnant woman!

Every time you add a couple of minutes
to my birth
remind us that the measurement of pain endures -
talk about how early in the morning it was;
how afraid you were
just eighteen and craving cherries
already out of season.

You know that same poem where you tell my daughter
she ought to be grateful for the women's movement
because now she can have an epidural,
dream of what she wants to be -
achieve it-
and never have to have cat stitches after birth
or worry about not having a job to go back to after the baby.

The problem for me is
I cannot write that poem
because I am caught up in thinking about you
the face of my mother
born in March
between Winter and Spring
just after the war

noticing that you still color Easter eggs
but not your hair.

I search for a metaphor
for the care and design that went into your life;
for the moments we have no words for.
 But my mind wanders, elongates itself
in the swing shifts of the un-metaphoric

and I drop into the moody voiceless
untrivial part of our experience.

I can't help myself
I am obsessively curious about the heart flowers
and the seeds of yearning
things that have little meaning in the common place
ordinary world

 So, I leave it as it is
in that light which lights the longer light
setting across my daughter's face
and peel an orange
while you laugh at the joke of social security.

That Break-with-Reality Episode

In the middle of the night
a door opens
spontaneously in your mind
and you stumble over
that tiny threshold
of reason
between gray dark and darker dark
to walk with ghosts
and demons
on the other side of sensibility.

Erratic, manic, and inflated
are all words
used to describe your way
of living
somewhere between the pit
of depression
and the wild fuck
of a stranger;

somewhere between the high
of meth
and a pill popping
prayer request
is your floating soul.

And, I know
what you're going to tell me
about this "condition"
but I don't
define you by that end
of reality
as we know it.

I remember you
as true love,
everlasting and bright
as a star.

Chanting in Blood Languages

I paint my face with dirt,

count the cycles of the moon

and wait cat-like

on a dark desert highway

for your return.

The sky does not deliver

a message from the ancestors.

No holy men speak,

none emerge from the shadows

or burst from a star.

I silently mouth the wound

you've abandoned

me into.

I give myself up in ceremony

only to howl

the one long sound a dog

makes: loyal but lost.

It is not so different

from a ghost

who wanders in a cemetery

seeking fire

chanting in blood languages.

Had it Been Water

Or a rebellious bird singing in Carmen's opera
I might have slammed on the brakes
instead I am inside the pages of a stolen biography
craving a love story with a prompt.

Remember we rode our bikes past station x
and laughed at the naked drawings under the bridge.

We caught crawdads, then threw them back.
We slid down the dirt hills on cardboard.
We flew kites until the trees stole them from us.

We imagined time was a marble in our hands.

You'd think by now you'd trust my love
is more than nana's coffee and short bread cookies.
It's more than playing in the bird bath and stacking legos.

Looking into your eyes every time is an ode
to the dark planets.

Leave of Absence

All of my life I have slept with you inside of me
not knowing that one day, mysteriously, you would leave.

And, I have held your secrets like the kiss of Eve,
the sleeping fish and Mary Magdalene.

I could not predict how somewhere between the gargoyles,
and desert rose, the cult of you would cease.

Faintly, I recall a conversation of conflicted horoscopes
but it was so brief, it could have been about palmistry.

I might blame it on the old crones jealous in gossip
who kept trying to steal the breath of you from my lips.

Or maybe it was early in the morning when your soul slipped
from my dry skin like a girl going to meet a lover.

Still, I wonder if it was all at once, or just slowly
through my feet, as if you thought I wouldn't notice.

Prayers at the Crossroads

Not everyone is filled with the hopes of sugar baked stories
and not all roads lead to the path of happiness.

I searched for you inside the heartbeat of geography
as a raptor circling to find the gauntlet.

At the crossroads, you laid sparkling in the sun
bleeding out as the hero you always wanted to be

cut on broken arrowheads
shattered glass, and blood rum.

I wished that I had wished for something else -
that I had been kinder, and less absorbed with myself.

I longed for other things too: an eagle whistle and honeysuckle,
mystic verses known only in the ancient caves of our ancestors.

I wished for tambourines, mandolins and abstract paintings.
I prayed for your resurrection. I prayed for your amnesia.

Lost Child

How I lost you, I am still not sure.

I keep going back through the photographs,
the facts, gathering all the data
to prove you were here...

I was there

    all along, for all of it, every thing

so this could not be the truth:

that you are lost

    (gone)

even though you are standing right in front of me

and
I am looking right into the dark center
                                  of your eyes.

Our Lady of the Lost Children

my little lambs sleep in dark alleys
fold themselves behind truck stops and gas stations

wash their hair with hand soap
in opium-stained bathrooms

busk for cash, fly signs on guitars
missing strings, carry man-slave mandolins

shave with shards of glass
huddle under bridges to dodge hurricanes

tiny ants on journeys toward nugatory destinations
hobo jungles and moonshine camps

my darling street urchins with face tattoos
and black fingernails search for rock pillows

crumble like pulverized kingdoms
into ruins, smashed torsos without heads

drink from brown paper bags
fish and fumble through empty bottles

gutter punks, rail riders, rainbow dopes, travelers
partly drowning, half soiled in slag

you listen through a stethoscope
bollixed that I breathe

my blood is their blood, my bones
are their bones, my light is their light

Published in Fractured Poetics, a poetry anthology published by Social Design, Inc, 2018.

This is what I inherited from you...

This is what I have inherited from you:
children of the lake,
flamingos with red tipped wings,
storybook witches,
egg thieves,
Egyptian Queens who are dead
in crocodile infested rivers,
and a soul filled with salt.

I no longer enter the moss-covered cave
of open teeth and shadows
where chimerical stories are told
or listen for the moonlight birds
that perch inside the magnolia trees
or follow the scent of gardenias blooming
after a night of ghosts.

Recalibration has left me with scars
in the forest of my life.

There are bones under my feet
masks on the ground,
(things I do not own)
and my children call out for you:
their echo is the echo of ancestors.

Naked on the Boulevard

It is more like the noise
a bullet makes
when it penetrates a window
to open everything
and shatter your vision.
We knew
of guns and gangs
as we walked
through a maze of broken reality
lit up with our poems.
Because the sky was clear
and a love song
played in the background...
It's not that the lyrics mattered
but how they made
us feel as our heads caught
on fire. Depending
on where you walk,
how your foot
sounds on the pavement,
words can easily slip,
get lost or smothered. Sometimes
they reverberate.
You told me how a verse changes
when it hits a hard object
or is struck by one. Velocity
delivers or breaks us
before we feel the wind touch
our skin. Your mouth
was smiling - with the screams
and sirens all around us -
you kept talking. I was too late...

before I started
my story was crushed
like a gangster's face into a wall.
And, here I am
naked on the boulevard
with the only feeling you ever intended
for me to know.

Nothing Except Opera

I never wrote the final song.
The love letters
did not turn into a melody

or float across the river
in a wood carved boat waving a white flag
or have a singing mermaid.

Meanwhile, he spills his alcohol, leaves
wine stains on coffee tables,
along with dirty socks on living room floors.

He craves a swift heroic death
where he does not have to accommodate anyone
and his speech is a legend.

In between suffocating words, he smokes
to hides the black circles under his eyes
and he lies on the sofa like a spent race horse.

Under my feet are crushed ashes;
my lungs are full of second-hand smoke,
and I have got nothing except opera.

My mythologies are violet blue,
a history of sperm-streaked sheets
and destroyed fruit.

Babies have lived inside of me, one died,
yet somehow, I turn everything holy
even when I am motionless.

I am the woman he is obsessing about,
a witch-dragon, a mother-queen, a slut-goddess,
and he would like to tear my wings off.

Illusions of Grandeur

I read a poem written by a man
who confessed

in the end he wanted to be the God
of his x girlfriend's broken heart,
the creator and curator of her happiness
or unhappiness.

He wanted his x to know
that he could take whatever he desired
in dark alleys or plain daylight;
that he might elaborate on the sin
and pleasure of possession,
drag out gritty details,
as if he could chain and unchain
love like a dog.

He was counting on her silence;
on her willingness
to play the victim and act innocent
because he thought she need it
to be accepted by society, to feel "belonging."

Except last night she was reading a story
about a man who discovered love in prison
while he was chained to a wall -
beaten, scraped, and torn from his bones.
He realized that to love or hate,
the freedom to choose,
that was the thing which made him human.

If the poet dares to think she is a ruined city
or a shattered woman,
because he gave into weakness
and fell prey to the seduction of his ego
or because she loved him once,
then he is kidding himself.

If he were not so busy trying to be God
he would see that she carries her cave
like a panther dark into the night, faceless.
She cannot be fully known.

He might finally understand
in every woman he is still enslaved.

Biography of a Stone

She sits like a rock outside my office window
between the glass and a trash can
to shade herself from the sun.

A conical tattered hat faded to a pale indigo
limits her sight behind eyes pounded flat
under the weight of opinions and pedantic ideas.

Scars like coins and crumpled notes fall out of pockets.
Streaked and riveted is her face into an expression
I do not have words for.

Her knees are bent to her chest,
with holes in checkered pants and dirty socks,
exposed through ripped shoes, broken by miles.

She speaks without words to a stash of sugar packages,
and suddenly turns to look into the glass.
Does she notice her reflection or feel mine?

In her granite eyes, I see there are advantages
to being a stone. Sleeping under rose bushes
and fighting the god of unmerciful winds

that carve her into beauty with shadow and light
chiseled by asphalt pillows, and marked
by the water of tears.

Painted in cave walls,
and young enough to be someone's daughter,
she is the house of skulls and eternity.

Slaughter Bone Oracle

Everyone is writing their own book
of the dead
and conjuring spirits.

It is not enough that the Egyptians
started the trend
and the Tibetans perfected it
or that the Africans called us
back to our origins.
It is not enough that my shadow
stopped breathing
and I etched the contents of who I am
deep inside
where I could stop the bleeding.

I wish to set the record straight.

Yes, there is a spiral of patterns
in my bones:
a spectrum of stories
like black ants
that stain the marrow.

Yes, I walked for miles
in tunnels I created in my own mind
and hid in the heart cave.

Yes, I have walked thru the gypsy oracle
the blood oracle, the tarot, and all the ungodly barren lands
and witnessed stars pinned haphazardly
to the exposed raw parts of the soul,
followed incomplete signs and listened to the broken songs
while trying to turn it all into art.
So, before your mind wanders
in search of flaws,

especially to the part
where bones crack and split,
and secrets spill out...

you have to ask yourself:
who throws the bones in the fire?

Then, I invite you to consider this:
a random confession will not be the answer you seek.

I met my Angel. I drank the Divine waters.
I belong to God now.

Apocalyptic Angel

She's sitting in a cafe
near a window
with a slight shadow on her neck
in a state of listening
pen alert -
a self-appointed ghost translator
more privileged
than any of her readers imagine
leaving behind a friend
who liked her when no one did
because it is a narrative
that does not fit
into the story
she intends to tell
thru the wounded deceased
a true grave robber
a thief of spirit songs
she resurrects mass hangings
and dog eating
histories from plantations
she has never seen
as she was raised in California sunlight
on a diet of her mother's piano lessons
reading Gatsby
taking elite trips to Paris
harboring an obsession for Colette
and pale chain-smoking men
quoting Nabokov by candle light
she has crushed her real life
into a selective truth
buried her former lovers
in a dirt of lies
(no one publishes that)

now she claims to know the weight
of chains she never wore
the sounds of screams
and vomit tossed overboard
histories she steals
crafts into prose sermons
like the preacher's daughter she is
drafting metaphors
from cotton
passing it for scripture
in the designer clothes
of superiority.

Vacant as the Sky

High above my ordinary life
the sky is a witness.
The moment is average
& the thought of you
is a cloud passing by.
All I find to explain
my lack luster attitude
is a word like *bewilderment*.
I too ask myself
why I bought the story of us.

Something random
& ultimately unknowable

like a poetry book
I carried home one night
clutching it to my heart.

I thought it held
the promise of transformation
& destiny
only to discover the pages
were blank.

One Hundred and One Poems Later

This is how we say "good-bye"
one hundred and one poems later
and without the moon's
cliche of light
or a tidal wave drowning us
in blue sorrows.

It is the absence of you
though you've scarcely left.
I know you've packed
your hopes into someone's trunk
without reflection
about where you'll end up.

The night unfolds its long darkness
before me
with ridiculous thoughts
about how you have already
forgotten us.

I am tempted to be a jerk
just to be sure
that I am remembered
since the cruel
are who you love best,
then I can prove I am worthy
of your loving scorn.

You replace everyone
with someone like a love junkie
and rewrite every poem
like a Jack Kerouac
with a notebook
of scratched out names.

I refuse to be a ghost
or become those recycled words
because it takes courage
to burn with real love
even when it appears dead.

I will keep the best
of us
pressed like orange blossoms
in a book
to honor how our hearts
we're once so close
that they could hear
the secrets

in the darkest hour
before
we turned our backs
to one another.

Floating in the Dark

I am accidentally here swimming in a metaphysical past
because I had a dream last night you were extending a hand to me.

Folklore about vampires that wander from their graves
without broken bones will not stop me
from the discovery of the moon sutras only the dead can speak.

I confess it is the promise of stardust after the bullfights
and red dresses that causes me to unbind my heart
unravel the mystery from the book of parables and seek serenity.

I cannot deny we fell apart the way flowers fall from branches
and your voice disappeared into the earth.

Let the gypsies moan their melodies about the deaths of sword swallowers
and pixies lost in oblivion. Let the midnight carnival dance
on to the raven's song in pantomime with tree spirits and enchantments.

The world is upside down besotted with its wounded dignity
dressed in vermilion and wild at heart
but the moon like the truth cannot be stolen.

I continue to write in water about our love,
see how brilliant its light is floating in the dark.

Meeting You in Jiangxi

In a salted state of body
I stand in this temple
between heaven and earth
listening for your voice
to curve with the land
as a red song that rises
over gloomy stones
polished naked as silence:
I cut ties with darkness
to scatter your ashes.

A Six-Winged Seraph Came to Earth

This is the day, the time, the hour
that I stop; that I lay down the sword

quit fighting and stop giving penance
for the cruelties inflicted on my body.

I heard a fairytale. Or maybe a Bible tale.
A story anyway you tell it. A myth maybe.

A six-winged seraph came to earth.

Someone named Mikhail Vrubel painted her portrait.
She must be important. I dream of her now.

Either way. I will stop apologizing for the jagged
fragments and scars on my hips.

I will keep the blue parts of my dark nights
and the pieces of me that stopped breathing.

The parts that hid under the bed.

I will keep the chunks of myself that dropped
all over the floor. A wounded animal.

Not angelic. Like I was supposed to be.
I lost my way. Between liver and spleen.

My heart burst out suddenly
and bled all over the country

when I least expected it to, like an unruly child
throwing up in the middle of the night.

Strangers pray. My mother prays.
I live off their prayers. I pray.

I light candles. I have an altar. Deer antlers.
Bobcat skulls. Jesus candles. Mary.

More angel paintings. Michelangelo. Raphael.

A crown fell from the sky, a little misshapen.
I heard only the silence of stars.

may the books of sky open

for you
with a gift of sunlight

to cherish and hold close to your heart
chanting the names of Angels

asking for the revelation of mysteries
like a map in a field of flowers

ephemeral in full bloom
white and blue as Mary Magdalene
born of morning:
the weeping fire and rose of a wounded soul
to encircle you in beauty

and when you find yourself
caught between seasons
may you choose to surround yourself
                in Divine warmth

Time to Give My Heart Away

Love, it is time to give my heart away.

Not because you have left
or are unwanted
but simply because you have soaked
though my bones
with each movement
and poured out to the earth at my feet

like the river that overflows
I am swollen in the sweet rush of you
with boundaries erased.

My soul is a fool
night after night, I sleep in the essence of you
more than a feeling, deeper than a memory
greater than any hope

but you are worth it,
so now it is time to share this love
with the world...

as you said, It is for everyone...
if I write it for you.

Published in Gained Loss, Kreative South Africa, 2008

The Song of the Living

The song of the living is my journey with you.
Do not stop looking or seeking
the skies are not just constellations or predictions.

The road is not just a thief of souls.

It is more than blood and tears
or scaring ourselves with wicked ink
and twigs.
It is more than cold bones sleeping
on the pavement
and flying signs at the gas station.
It is more than dumpster diving
and searching for someone's precious leftovers
under busted street lights.

It is more than the blisters, bruised toes,
broken guitar strings,
and the 5150.
It is more than forgotten names,
betrayed friends,
stolen identities,
and people that were left behind.

It is the singing, and the giving,
and the pulse of a tune,
the blues of a vein
until there is no more voice left to sing.

It is the receiving of Grace
under bridges,
listening to the mosquitoes
of everything insane
while waiting for the trains.

It is the roadside shrines
made of plastic flowers
and candles, and little Mementos
to a life that was brief
but important to someone.

It is the loving and the dancing,
and the shine in your eyes;
it is your hand in my hand
until our hands fall away
from one another
like hearts unbraided.

It is the way that we walk together
for miles in silence
through deserts,
through storms,
through tornadoes,
through snow,
through rain,
across state-lines
through Devils Lake
through the unmerciful blistering sun,
until our faces are cracked,
and it is the smile, and the laughter

for no reason at all

other than we're caught in a sandstorm
taking shelter under a rock,
talking about the way we were born.
How we've lived longer
than we ever imagined we would.

It is your life and my life
woven together
for no reason other than
we found each other
on the road.
This is something that no one
can explain,
it's not even written
in the cartography
of the stars.

In Search of a Gypsy Love Poem

In the beginning...

I wanted to write a love poem
about a gypsy

with a voice that rises like the sun
in your blood,

a real Sunday sweetheart
to kiss you:

a true free-spirit
as a messenger of passion

dancing in the blue temple
and smelling of amber

with something to wrap you in hope,
charming as her sexy eyes,

a sultry mythology.

I searched for the flower child
and the bohemian

in myself

hoping to find a tender curiosity
and invent a rhyme

that saves vagabonds, outlaws
and abandoned cities.

Surely you wouldn't be satisfied
with a forgotten goddess

or one who shelters the ghosts
like a muted swan

weaving night flowers
in your sleep.

I discovered a tart, a tramp,
a wandering nomad

with a pocket of angel wings
and no confession

other than she carries her soul
as a melody

and wears her halo
better than a queen.

She sang these words to me:

>   You have to teach your heart
>   to start over.

By Now the Light has Faded

The holy rage has gone down
with the sun of anger
and the story of enlightenment
is writing your name
through a sliver of moon
so in this moment of reflection
the ashes of burnt of hearts
are carried by the wind
to settle in the deep waters
of the unborn.

The Light the Angels Speak Of

It doesn't interest me if I am to be dust, ashes
or thrown into the fire many times.
I don't want to be a shooting star or blaze of wonder
or to be a self-righteous one that pontificates
or to scream from a roof top.

I can't imagine being a sleepy planet
or wasting my days counting the minutes.

I was born to live from the center of life,
to walk among all people…the wounded, creative, loving,
offering whatever I have to offer.

I am the life that melts while it's living
I am the love of God,
and the light angels speak of.

The Unveiling

We are here together in Grace.

In the same light as dreamers and lovers
In the same cave as mystics, sculptors, and poets.

Together we circle the forgotten children, abandoned souls,
the broken spirits, the unhoused and neglected.

We call on our ancestors who have gone before us
in great courage, and those who are faithful.

We honor them.

We ask ourselves, what does it mean to be alive today?
We ask this because we know there is a mystery in the heart

of this journey, and there is pain, and sorrow, and mercy.
There is magic, and yearning, and affection

unfolding from the center of our being
as we remember that we will not allow death to silence

our gratitude, our hope, or the wonder
we feel as we witness the mirrored mosaic of Love

in this moment of reflection.

Together in generosity under the same sun
we kiss; and under the same moon, we bleed.

The floods, curses and storms come to devour
all our brothers and sisters, our mothers, and fathers.

We dance without wings, make deals with God;
prick our own fingers on the roses we planted.

Let us forgive each other as friends, as lovers, as radicals
and call in the Divine, as we lift our eyes skyward

to pray.

Author's NOTES & ACKNOWLEDGMENTS:

The poems published in this collection were written between 2000-2022. Several of them first appeared in various anthologies between 2007-2022 and I have gathered them together here in this collection. Please considered looking up these anthologies, if they are still in print, as many of the authors are excellent writers, and it was an honor to be included with them.

- Feeling is First, Social Design, 2007 ("By Now the Has Faded")
- Alehouse Press, Number 1, Poetry on Tap, 2007 ("Meeting You in Jiangxi")
- Memoir (and) Journal 2008 ("under the Ribs")
- 34th Parallel, 2007 ("In San Francisco with My Father")
- Gained Loss, Kreative South Africa, 2008 ("Love's Sanctuary," "Time to Give My Heart Away.")
- Flax to Gold, Kreative South Africa, 2009 ("A Love Story Inside the Structure of Color," "In the Field of My Soul.")
- An African Legend, White Lions & Leopards, SA Private, 2010 ("Born from the Tear of Lions," "Leopard Song," "Faded Heiroglyphs")
- An African Legend, White Lions & Marine Mammals, SA Private 2011 ("Stained with Salt," "Angel Heart Resurrected," "Sleep in the Sea Tonight with Me.")
- Keepers of the Mystical White Lions & White Bison, edited by Maurice Fernandez, 2012 ("Our Hearts are Listening")
- Aquillrelle, Anthology, 2011 ("Meditation")
- Some Voices Sing, An Anthology of Hope; Blue Catharsis Publishing, 2016 ("Another Kind of Purple," Ash," and "Bee Keeper")
- Women, Mujeres, IXOQ: Revolutionary Visions, Conocimientos Press, LLC, 2017 ("Skyjacked")
- Fractured Poetics, Social Designs, 2018 ("Our Lady of the Lost Children")
- Poetic Velocity, Social Designs, 2019 ("blue Lanterns in midsummer")

- The Wide-Open Sky, Anthology, Kevin Watt, 2020 ("San Francsico Jangle")
- IMPRESSIONS & EXPRESSIONS Anthology of Contemporary Poetry, edited by Amita J. Sanghavi, 2021 ("Eating Marigold," "Becoming a Falcon," "Alabaster," "Dreamcatcher," "Lotus in the Mud," "Unabbreviated," "Gutter Punk," "Hobo Cavalcade," "Chanting in Blood Languages")

www.ingramcontent.com/pod-product-compliance
Lightning Source LLC
Chambersburg PA
CBHW070122100426
42744CB00010B/1896